The Book Of Children Grandma's Words of Wisdom
By
Pat Cher

Illustrations Sonya Robinson

Dear Grandma,

Is it true God loves me? I don't understand.
Me

Dear Little One,

That's how I think of you as my dear little one (You're not so little anymore, I know). Yes, God made you. He made you because he loves you so very much.

\   Think of someone you love; your Mom, Dad, your dog. God loves you much more than you could ever love anyone. God is Love. Awesome isn't it?

I love you too, but I can't beat God at loving, that's what He is and what He does.

He loves you bigger than the sky, bigger than the stars, bigger than the whole world.

He loves me that much too.

Lots of Love,
    Grandma

Dear Grandma,

What does it mean to have a strong or a weak character?

Dear Little One,

That's a very good question, and I remember wondering about that too, as I was growing up. Character has to do with spirit, and how you react to people and situations.

You might want to think of it as trying to do things in the right way. Just as there are people who are stronger than others, so there are people who are stronger in doing things that are right.
For example, it's sometimes easier to lie than to tell the truth, but the strong person tells the truth.
If you want to have a

strong character you have to practice being strong in difficult situations. Just as a person who wants to get strong in body has to exercise and keep active.

Love you so much,
Grandma

Dear Grandma,
How do I become a kind person?
Me

Dear Little One,
You are kind already, but if you want to become kinder, practice doing something kind every day. The more you practice the better you become at it.
Love you,
Grandma

Dear Grandma,

How do I talk to God? Does he talk back? What do I say when I talk to Him?

Me

Dear Little One,
    You can talk to God in any way you want. You can talk out loud or just in your heart. You can talk to Him when you're

alone or when you're in a crowd. You can talk to him about anything; about your friends, about what makes you happy, about what makes you sad, about what you did today or about what you want to do tomorrow.
It's easy to talk to God. Yes, He does answer, but you have to listen. He answers in different ways. He can answer in your heart, or you can

find the answer in the things or people around you.
Listening to God takes practice, because we can't see him, and we sometimes don't wait or don't look for his answer. I've been practicing for a long time and I'm still not very good at listening to Him.

Love you, Grandma

Dear Grandma,
 What's a soul? Do I have one? What does it look like?
 Me

Dear Little One,
 Everyone has a soul. God lovingly made it in the palm of His hand. Awesome, isn't it?
 We can't see our souls just as we can't see God. Our souls were made more beautiful than

anything we know and it's our job to keep them beautiful. Every time we are unkind or unloving our soul gets a little smear or a spot (at least that's the way I picture it).

    When someone hurts you, you also get a spot. You can imagine how spotty your soul can get. Isn't that sad? But, God is so good that if you tell Him you're sorry, he'll make it new again.

The spots someone threw at you (when they hurt you) go away when you forgive them. Sounds easy, doesn't it? Remember God loves you It doesn't matter what you do, He's ready to make your soul as beautiful as it was on the day He made it.

You're special to me,
Grandma

Dear Grandma,

Why do people get old?
What does it feel like?
Me

Dear Little One,

I once was told that growing old was a gift, a priviledge. Not everyone is chosen to grow old. Growing old means becoming an elder.

When you become an elder you pass on what you know to others just like I'm trying to do for you.
Some people pass on special skills, others pass on knowledge.
It's important to those growing up that they have someone to teach them, someone to turn to, when they don't have all the answers.
Imagine if you had to

learn everything by yourself with no help.

Love you forever,
Grandma

Dear Grandma,
    Why do people have to die?
                    Me

Dear Little One,
    People die when their time here is finished. It could happen anytime to anyone. It is a frightening thought isn't it? But, it doesn't have to be. We have to thank God every day for the time He has given us

here, and we have to try to spend that time wisely.

God is so much wiser than we are. He loves us so very much too. When we die we get to see Him and it is only then that we realise how much He loves us.
Dying is like going to another world, going on a trip. We become more like God. We see all our friends and relative who

haven't died, but they don't see us until it's their turn to join God's heavenly kingdom.
His world is much more beautiful than what we have here. There is no pain, no suffering and everyone is kind and gentle. It's a very good and safe place.

Hugs and kisses,
Grandma

Dear Grandma,
My friend really hurt my feelings. What should I do?
Me

Dear Little One,
You must be very sad. A friend can hurt us so much more than someone else. Remember what I told you about forgiveness. You have to forgive your friend so you'll feel right inside.

Those spots on your soul always make you feel uncomfortable. Forgiving is not easy. You have to ask God who is awesome and your great friend to help you. He'll help make the friendship right again, if you ask Him.

God is so happy when you're loving. It reminds me of the story of the butterfly. I often think that when we do the ordinary things in life, we

are like the caterpillar
and still loved by God,
but that when we do
something with love, in
God's eyes we soar like
butterflies but
butterflies more brilliant
and beautiful than we
can imagine.
Try to be a butterfly
every day.

You are special to me and
to God,
Grandma

Dear Grandma,

What do I do when
people make me angry?
                      Me

Dear Little One,

You have to forgive them.
Your questions remind me
of when I'm driving down
the street and someone
cuts me off or drives
dangerously. I really feel

like calling them all kinds of names. Instead, I remember that God loves them too and I say a prayer for them. I feel tricky doing that because I think that the devil enjoys seeing me angry. It's fun to do the opposite of what he wants me to do.

Love always,
Grandma

Dear Grandma,
    How do you be a friend?
        Me

Dear Little One,
    Friends make life so much more interesting. You're asking me a very good question. It tells me you already know friends are important. Always remember that people (friends) are much more important than things.

I have to tell you a true story about someone I know. He has a very special friend. They have known each other since they were in baby carriages. They have not always lived close to each other but they have always kept in touch.

Now both live close by and they call each other at least twice a day. They do volunteer work together. Their friendship has lasted their whole life so far. Imagine that?

    How have they done this? They argue a lot. Neither one hesitates about telling the other off. I think the important thing is that they don't hold a grudge. If one of them is mad over something by the time they talk to each other the next day it's forgotten. They forgive and then it's gone.

They are also there for each other if either needs help in anyway.

I hope you can find a friend like that or even two or three. Friends are so important.

To be a true friend you have to follow God's example. He's always there when you need Him. If you want to be a friend you have to be there for that person when it feels good and when it doesn't feel so good. In a difficult situation when you're not sure of what to do you can always ask yourself, what would God do?

You're special to me,
Grandma

Dear Grandma,

My friend is very sad.

What should I do?
Me

Dear Little One,

    When our friends are sad it makes us sad too. Don't be afraid to show your friend that you feel his pain. If you can, do little things, special things that show you care. It could be sharing a special treat, doing a favour or standing by your friend in a difficult moment.

Sometimes it helps if you just touch the other person on the shoulder or on the hand, just a little touch to show that you are there for them. Sometimes a loving touch can do wonders. Try it you'll see.

The best kind of friend is the one who tries to help you when you are sad.

Love you tender,
Grandma

Dear Grandma,
    My friend does so many things better than me. How can I be better?
Me

Dear Little One,
    There will always be someone who will be better than you at something. What you have to do is find out what you are very good at doing.
    Here's something to

help you. When you were born the angels thanked God for you. They knew that God had made you a perfect fit to everyone you would meet. Try to discover that secret.

How? It takes a lifetime for most people. Every night this week, before you go to bed, ask your angel or God to show you one of your gifts.

Also, thank God often

for having made you. Say, "Thank you, God, for making me special in your eyes."

He did make you special. You are the apple of His eyes. Make sure you also thank God for your friend. Treasure your friend because to have a friend is very special.

Love you every day,
Grandma

Dear Grandma,
 I'm having problems with a bully. What can i do?
 Me

Dear Little One,
 First, I will pray for you and for the person who is being a bully. I would like you to pray about it too. Ask God to show you what you must do. Pray that God will change his heart. I think

the bully must be a very unhappy person. Maybe he wants everyone else to be unhappy too.

    Secondly, I want you to remember a very important truth. People only have as much power (control) as you and others are willing to give them. What does that mean to you in this situation? The bully is trying to control you by making you afraid. Every

time you show you are afraid, he wins. Bullies pick on those weaker than they are, people they can control. Now the difficult part... How do you break the control he has over you? Here are some suggestions.
-Don't show you're afraid, turn and walk away.
-Find friends to hang around with maybe others who are being picked on. There is strength in

numbers.

-Have special activities in your group. Maybe bully will want to join. Only let him join on the condition that the bullying stops. If they continue, don't let him be part of the group.

-Form a secret society with one or two very good friends, try to find something good about the bully, compliment him about it. When he isn't bullying try to find ways

of being nice to him.
-Talk to an adult, a teacher, your parents, a friend's parents, an uncle or an aunt, someone you like and trust) about your problems and see if together you can come up with a solution.

Love you lots,
Grandma

Dear Grandma,

My teacher asked me a question today, and I didn't tell her the truth. I told a lie. What should I do?

Me

Dear Little One,

    You must feel sad. I know you don't make a habit of lying. Do you know why most people lie? They lie mostly because they are afraid. So I think that maybe you were afraid to tell your teacher the truth. If you told the truth, what do you think would have happened? Now think about it another way. If your teacher discovers that you told a lie. How will you feel? It's the same as telling a friend a lie. Once, they know you lied, it's difficult for them to trust you again.

    I know you are brave, and don't need to tell a lie. You are also brave enough to go tell your teacher you lied. You don't have to do it in front of the class, just ask the teacher if you can see her at recess or after class. Remember, to say you're sorry. The lying not only hurt you, it hurt your teacher too.

Here's something a wise man once said:

You know what it's like when you find out a friend is a liar? Whatever he says, after that, sounds false, however true it may be." --Jean Giraudoux

Remember, if you lie one time, it's much easier to lie a second time and then it could become a habit. The other thing about a lie, we sometimes have to lie again to keep it going, and it takes a good memory to remember all the lies. Mark Twain said it best; "If you tell the truth, you don't have to remember anything."

So today I'll say a little prayer for you. As for you, be sure to ask

God to help you do the right thing, I'm sure that with such a powerful friend you'll know just what to do.

Love you very much,

Grandma

Thank you for reading The Book of Children, I hope you, your children, grandchildren enjoyed it,

If you've enjoyed the book, please write a comment. Positive feedback helps me keep writing. Leave reviews on Amazon...

http://goo.gl/ZtsMxD

Note: The illustrations in the book and the book cover are by Sonya Robinson

Pat Cher, author
Mi'kmaq Song on
Amazon at …
http://goo.gl/JhQB7B

www.ingramcontent.com/pod-product-compliance
Lightning Source LLC
LaVergne TN
LVHW010019070426
835507LV00001B/5